KICK IT!

Nick Toczek goes swimming and buys things on eBay. He's a poet, magician, storyteller, puppeteer, novelist, comedian, local radio DJ and bald dad. He breeds lizards and likes living in Bradford because he was born there.

There's lots more about him on the Internet. Try putting his name into a good search engine such as Google.

Alan Rowe has been working as an illustrator since he graduated from Kingston University. He lives in Sutton, Surrey, with his partner, who is also an illustrator, three children, two cats, two goldfish and a room full of toy robots. He supports Chelsea.

Kick It!
Football Poems

Nick Toczek

Illustrated by Alan Rowe

MACMILLAN CHILDREN'S BOOKS

First published 2002
by Macmillan Children's Books
a division of Macmillan Publishers Ltd
20 New Wharf Road, London N1 9RR
Basingstoke and Oxford
Associated companies throughout the world
www.panmacmillan.com

ISBN 978-0-330-39920-3

7 9 8

A CIP catalogue record for this book is available from the British Library.

Printed by Mackays of Chatham plc, Chatham, Kent.

Contents

For Eunice Doherty, my mum-in-law, who died in January 2002. We all miss you.

Wordplay

Play your pals at football.
Be in a play at school.
Learn to play the piano
But not to play the fool.

Get a new Playstation.
Play stubborn as a mule.
Play with fire, play it safe
Or play it by the rule.

Play together nicely
'Cos playing tricks is cruel.
Play and get excited
Or play it super-cool.

Play on everybody's nerves.
Play a game of pool.
Dream you'll be a player
Who'll play for Liverpool.

The Visitor

There in the goal mouth, between either post,
We sometimes see something . . . or someone, almost.
It's just a faint glow
But all of us know
It's Gordon the goalie's old ghost.

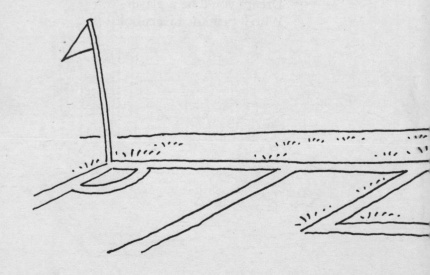

A Football is the Ball for Me

I don't want a bowling ball built like a brick
And volleyball is horri-ball, it gets on my wick.
I want a ball, a ball, a ball you can kick.

I wouldn't want to hit it with a wooden hockey-stick
And to chuck it at a wicket in cricket is sick.
I want a ball, a ball, a ball you can kick.

My superball'll bounce off a wall dead quick
But a ball so small ain't worth a flick.
I want a ball, a ball, a ball you can kick.

Though netball's cool and baseball's slick,
There's only one ball game they just can't lick.
I want a ball, a ball, a ball you can kick.

One ball I need. One ball I'd pick.
I don't want six for a juggling trick.
I want a ball, a ball, a ball you can kick.

There's just one game with which I click.
Football, through thin and thick.
Football wins my voting tick.
Football, or my name's not Nick . . .

  . . . but it is.
So I want a ball,
    a real ball,
        a proper ball,
            a ball you can kick.

The Football Family Man

I'm the finest fan
That football's had.
I've a football gran
With a football fad.
I've a football mother
And a football dad.
And my football brother
Has football bad.

With my football wife
In our football pad
To our football life
We football add
Two football daughters
And a football lad,
All football supporters,
All football mad.

We've football dogs,
They're football clad
In football togs
Like a football ad.
For our football ways,
We're football glad.
Without football days
We'd be football sad.

I'm a football man
Who's football mad.
I'm the finest fan
That football's had.
I'm the football family man.

When Do I Think About Football?

I start to think about football
Whenever I look at my bedroom wall –
I've soccer posters, soccer books,
And scarves and boots and kits on hooks.

I think about it in the bath
And walking down the garden path
And during breakfast, dinner and tea
And while I sit and watch TV.

I think about it elsewhere too,
Like in the kitchen and the loo,
And going up and down the stairs.
And football features in my prayers.

And I count goals instead of sheep
And dream of teams while I'm asleep,
And start again when I'm awake,
Then sitting in school, and during break.

And in assembly, singing a hymn,
And in the playground and the gym
It's football occupies my thoughts.
I never think of other sports.

It's why I reach most lessons late,
And why I'm told to concentrate,
'Cos football's all they'd probably find
If they could see inside my mind.

It's with me while I'm on my own
And while I'm talking on the phone,
Or standing waiting at a stop,
Or on a bus, or in a shop.

It comes with me on holiday,
Or to a friend's, or out to play.
And if I dwell on other things,
It always hovers in the wings.

And, come to think of it, right now
It's on my mind again, somehow . . .
Apart from which, I don't recall
Thinking of football much at all.

The Duty of a Football Poet

I feel it is my duty-oh
To praise the grace and beauty-oh
Of every dribble, every flick
And every tiny little kick
Encountered in Subbuteo.

Me 'n' My Magic Football Boots

We're in league, in cahoots

Me 'n' my magic
Me 'n' my magic
Me 'n' my magic football boots.

There's no other footwear suits.
In rhyming slang, my daisy roots,
Got no match, no substitutes.

Me 'n' my magic
Me 'n' my magic
Me 'n' my magic football boots.

Football chants and whoops and hoots
And wild applause and drums and flutes
And rattle clatters, whistle toots.

Me 'n' my magic
Me 'n' my magic
Me 'n' my magic football boots.

Watch which move each executes
Spot their separate attributes,
Left one tackles, right one shoots.

Me 'n' my magic
Me 'n' my magic
Me 'n' my magic football boots.

Funky Football

Sock it to me
Sock it to me
Sock-sock-soccer it

Root-ti-toot
Y'go shoot, shoot, shoot
Shoot, shoot, shoot
With your football boot

We're losing now
But let's get cute
And turn the tide
Like King Canute
Let's win this game
And reap the fruit
Clean as a whistle
Clear as a flute

Root-ti-toot
Y'go shoot, shoot, shoot
Shoot, shoot, shoot
With your football boot

So sock it to me
Sock it to me
Sock-sock-soccer it

Root-ti-toot
Y'go shoot, shoot, shoot
Shoot, shoot, shoot
With your football boot

It's in the bag
The game's a beaut
It's a long loud laugh
It's hoot, hoot, hoot
So keep your cool
Be resolute
Goals are what
We'll execute

Root-ti-toot
Y'go shoot, shoot, shoot
Shoot, shoot, shoot
With your football boot

So sock it to me
Sock it to me
Sock-sock-soccer it

Root-ti-toot
Y'go shoot, shoot, shoot
Shoot, shoot, shoot
With your football boot.

Football Time

Put on your boots, your shirt, your shorts.
It's time to play the king of sports,
An ancient game, by all reports,
Which even occupied the thoughts
Of Jason and the Argonauts
And Roman soldiers in cohorts
Who shivered in their northern forts.

Put on your boots, your shirt, your shorts.
It's time to play the king of sports,
Its fans are folk of many sorts
From farms and towns and coastal ports
And prison cells and royal courts
And rocket-ships . . . yes, astronauts
And aliens with heads like warts,
Their bodies built like juggernauts
With things like limbs, though each contorts.

Put on your boots, your shirt, your shorts.
It's time to play the king of sports,
That almost everyone supports
Except the oddball who just snorts
Then strides out on to tennis courts
Or croquet lawns where he cavorts
With colleagues of the strangest sorts,
The sorts you'd choose as last resorts.

But we've got boots and shirts and shorts.
Come on . . . let's play the KING of sports!

Team Photo

Some stand, some squat, some sit, none laugh.
Neat rows, neat hair, neat kit, the faff.
The pose with folded arms is naff.
The team, the boss, the chosen staff.
The formula for a photograph.

Football Grounds

You take no corners in a round ground,
Get in cheap to a pound ground,
Sing and chant in a sound ground,
Claim the game in a found ground,
Get rained off in a drowned ground,
Shop around in a towned ground,
Have a ball in a gowned ground,
Play for laughs in a clowned ground,
Grimly, though, in a frowned ground,
Briefly, in a knock-around ground,
Tie the game in a bound ground,
Feel the heat in a browned ground,
Quench your thirst in a downed ground,
Dig the past in a mound ground,
Deeply in a profound ground,
Run with the pack in a hound ground,
Watch the time in a wound ground,
Turn to dust in a ground ground.

How to Become the Player-Manager of a Poem

Take all you've seen and thought and said
And kick the words around your head.
Play with them on a paper pitch.
Select a few, the rest you'll ditch.

Position the best to form your team
And tackle your theme and match your scheme.
Then lead them clearly, nice and loud,
Out in front of the waiting crowd.

The World's First Football

Where did the very first football fall?
Did it land in the land of the Neanderthal?
Was it sold in a Flintstone shopping mall?
Or an ancient Athenian market stall?
Or in any other early urban sprawl?

Where did the very first football fall?
Did Jesus of Nazareth kick it to Paul?
Did Confucius bounce it off the Chinese Wall?
Was it all-weather leather? Was it large or small?
Was it in a proper game or a free-for-all?

Where did the very first football fall?
Does any old history book recall?
Can you find it on a pyramid in hieroglyphic scrawl?
Did the Romans kick it around in Gaul?
Or a Viking crew in an ancestral hall?

Where did the very first football fall?
At the feet of a Zulu two metres tall?
At the little boots of Leprechauns in County Donegal?
Or was it wrought in rubber by a native of Nepal?
Or did they kick a coconut in sunny Senegal?

So where did the very first football fall?
Does anyone have any idea at all ...? No!

Kick a Ball

Kick a ball, kick a ball
Kick a ball in Montreal
Kick a ball, kick a ball
Kick a ball in Cornwall
Kick a ball, kick a ball
Kick a ball in Bengal
Kick a ball, kick a ball.

Kick it when I come to call
Kick it up against a wall
Kick it big or kick it small
Kick it over there to Paul
Kick it in a free-for-all
Kick it if you've got the gall.

Kick a ball, kick a ball
Kick a ball in Montreal
Kick a ball, kick a ball
Kick a ball in Cornwall
Kick a ball, kick a ball
Kick a ball in Bengal
Kick a ball, kick a ball.

Kick it over something tall
Kick it down a waterfall
Kick it round the county hall
Kick in the shopping mall
Kick it fast or at a crawl
Kick it with a caterwaul.

Kick a ball, kick a ball
Kick a ball in Montreal
Kick a ball, kick a ball
Kick a ball in Cornwall
Kick a ball, kick a ball
Kick a ball in Bengal
Kick a ball, kick a ball

Kick a kick a kick a ball!

To Be a Star

Every fan
Dreams this dream
Scoring for
Their football team.

Goal on goal
Scheme of schemes
Rise through football's
Rich regime.

Oh to glow
Gleam and gleam
Rule the pitch
And glean esteem.

Hear the crowd
Scream and scream
Ecstasy
In the extreme.

Celebration
Streamers stream
Kiss the cup
And reign supreme.

Hit that height
Cream of cream
Topping soccer's
Academe.

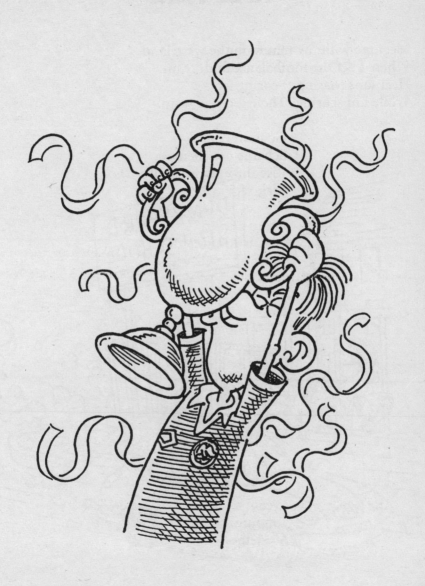

I'll Be Soccer

Meet me with my mates on the wasteland
Where I act the football ace and
Hear fans roaring
While I'm scoring.

Soon I'll leave my mates in the wasteland.
I'm gonna drive a flashy car.
I'm gonna dine on caviare.
I'm gonna smoke a fat cigar.
I'll be posh and lah-di-dah.
I'll be soccer
I'll be soccer
I'll be soccer's superstar.

Find me with my friends in assembly,
I pray one day I'll play at Wembley.
My daydream
Is a grade-A team.

Soon I'll leave my friends in assembly.
I'm gonna drive a flashy car.
I'm gonna dine on caviare.
I'm gonna smoke a fat cigar.
I'll be posh and lah-di-dah.
I'll be soccer
I'll be soccer
I'll be soccer's superstar.

Picture me with pals in the playground.
I pretend that we're on the way round
Grounds in Europe
Pushing our score up.

Soon I'll leave my pals in the playground.
I'm gonna drive a flashy car.
I'm gonna dine on caviare.
I'm gonna smoke a fat cigar.
I'll be posh and lah-di-dah.
I'll be soccer
I'll be soccer
I'll be soccer's superstar.

Chocolate, Cheese and the Birth of Football

That old Greek doc, Hippocrates,
(Pronounced to rhyme with chocolate cheese)
Once played in The Cup
In a game thought up
By some bright spark called Soccer-it-is.

Hippocrates, remembered as the 'Father of Medicine', and the philosopher, Socrates, both lived in Greece in the fifth century BC.

Never Put Noel in Goal

Oh, no! There goes another goal.
That must make it ten they stole.

Why do we suffer this terrible toll?
Because some fool put Noel in goal.

Oh, no! Not Noel.
He flaps around like a Dover sole.
We always get this rigmarole
Whenever we've got Noel in goal.

So who gave Noel that role?
Who put Noel in goal?
I bet they think they're drole.

Give 'em jail with no parole.
They must be round the pole.

Noel, Noel, pathetic prole,
Without one virtue to extol,
A sorry soul with no control.

Take a stroll, Noel.
Crawl back in your hole.
Quit the team, claim the dole.

A sightless mole
Would patrol our goal
Better, on the whole,
Than you, Noel.

A frightened foal
Could fill your role,
Or a water vole
Or a lump of coal.

If we enrol
A toilet bowl
I bet it plays better than you, Noel!

Winners . . .

We won the game!
We won the game!
With points to claim
And fans and fame.
And life became
A vivid flame
And all because
We won the game.

We won the game!
We won the game!
And now proclaim
The cup's our aim.
It's in the frame
And so's acclaim
And all because
We won the game.

. . . And Losers

We lost the game!
We lost the game!
Our tactics tame
Our tackles lame.
Our lousy aim
Has brought us shame
And all because
We lost the game.

We lost the game!
We lost the game!
The ref's to blame
So curse his name.
Now life, we claim,
Won't be the same
And all because
We lost the game.

Why Groundsmen Never Relax

We touchily patch up our pitches
Where too much match-action despatches grass patches
And batches of scratch-marks, where boots catch, carve ditches.

We're grouches because of these hitches:
Those patches and scratches and ditches
That all matches hatch on our pitches.

We've a hotch-potch of blotches, a richness of itches,
Much agony, ouches and stitches,
All actually brought on by these glitches
Due to passes and tackles and switches.

And it's match watching which is
What hatches our unnatural twitches.

Old Man United

From 1940s army camps
Comes the team led by my gramps –
A bunch of ancient, grumpy scamps.
Old Man United,
    Man United,
    Man United think they're champs.

Their pitch is floodlit by gas lamps,
Dull as a bulb that's just five amps.
They look like scarecrows, ghosts and tramps.
Old Man United,
    Man United,
    Man United think they're champs.

The kits they bought with clothing stamps,
Have patches, stitches, clips and clamps
From years of mending and revamps.
Old Man United,
    Man United,
    Man United think they're champs.

They can't climb steps, they all need ramps.
They're sensitive to draughts and damps.
Despite arthritis, coughs and cramps,
Old Man United,
    Man United,
    Man United think they're champs.

"Come on, United!" "Come on, Gramps!"
Old Man United,
    Man United,
    Man United think they're champs.

Saturday Evening

From Dundee to Dover
The games are all over
And those who have lost
Will be counting the cost . . .

I know it'll vex 'em
In Oldham and Wrexham.
At Clydebank and Clyde
They'll have cried and have cried.
They'll be glumly pathetic
At Charlton Athletic,
But moodily manly
At Accrington Stanley.

'Cos nobody likes to lose.
They stand there and stare at their shoes.
They're gob-smacked and gutted
Like they've been head-butted.
Life's not worth a carrot.
They're sick as a parrot
And struggle to cope with the news.

At Manchester City
They're full of self-pity.
At Port Vale they're pale,
At Alloa, sallower,
Sullen in Fulham.
Morose at Montrose,
And Bradford and Burnley
Just sulk taciturnly.

'Cos nobody likes to lose.
They stand there and stare at their shoes.
They're gob-smacked and gutted
Like they've been head-butted.
Life's not worth a carrot.
They're sick as a parrot
And struggle to cope with the news.

And down Grimsby Town
Oh, how grimly they frown!
And Partick and Chelsea
Grow sick and unhealthy,
While at Aston Villa
They're very much iller,
And it's really killing 'em
In Millwall and Gillingham.

'Cos nobody likes to lose.
They stand there and stare at their shoes.
They're gob-smacked and gutted
Like they've been head-butted.
Life's not worth a carrot.
They're sick as a parrot
And struggle to cope with the news.

In Barnsley and Barnet
They spit and say, "Darn it!"
At Preston North End
Now they're nobody's friend.
And down Crystal Palace
They bristle with malice,
While Reading and Rangers
Are dangers to strangers.

'Cos nobody likes to lose.
They stand there and stare at their shoes.
They're gob-smacked and gutted
Like they've been head-butted.
Life's not worth a carrot.
They're sick as a parrot
And struggle to cope with the news.

Some fans of Southend
Have just gone round the bend,
And they're less than delighted
At West Ham United.
And down-in-the-mouth
Up in Queen of the South
While they look like left overs
At poor Tranmere Rovers.

'Cos nobody likes to lose.
They stand there and stare at their shoes.
They're gob-smacked and gutted
Like they've been head-butted.
Life's not worth a carrot.
They're sick as a parrot
And struggle to cope with the news.

Not a grin or a smile
Around Plymouth Argyle,
While they fret and they frown
Down in Kettering Town.
They're crestfallen and pale
In Walsall and Rochdale,
And it's gone past a joke
For Doncaster and Stoke.

'Cos nobody likes to lose.
They stand there and stare at their shoes.
They're gob-smacked and gutted
Like they've been head-butted.
Life's not worth a carrot.
They're sick as a parrot
And struggle to cope with the news.

In York and Hull City
The talk isn't pretty,
While Torquay and Lincoln
Have taken to drinkin'.
You'll not find a jester
In Chester or Leicester –
They've got lots to bother 'em
And so've Notts and Rotherham.

'Cos nobody likes to lose.
They stand there and stare at their shoes.
They're gob-smacked and gutted
Like they've been head-butted.
Life's not worth a carrot.
They're sick as a parrot
And struggle to cope with the news.

They're not very merry
In Blackburn and Bury.
They're choking in Woking
Where no one is joking.
There's an air of despair
In the air over Ayr,
And the black cloud's a big 'un
That hangs over Wigan.

'Cos nobody likes to lose.
They stand there and stare at their shoes.
They're gob-smacked and gutted
Like they've been head-butted.
Life's not worth a carrot.
They're sick as a parrot
And struggle to cope with the news.

Scandal

The man's in a mess
Splashed in the press
Causing his fans
And his family distress.
What did he do?
It's easy to guess . . .
Should've said no,
Instead he said yes.
Greedy for more.
Now he's got less.
Waving goodbye
To soccer success.

Unlikely

Imagine an airbag of leather,
Which got kicked around in bad weather,
And became a game
To which thousands came
To spectate and get wet together.

Kick It, Kid!

That's their goal, chum, not a wicket.
We don't bowl, mate. This ain't cricket.
Ball control, pal. You can't lick it.

Kick it!
Kick it!
Kick it, kid!

Don't just stand there like a picket
Stuck in quicksand or a thicket.
Get in! Tackle him and nick it.

Kick it!
Kick it!
Kick it, kid!

Don't just lob or chuck or flick it.
Go for it, now. That's the ticket!
See that net? That's where you stick it.

Kick it!
Kick it!
Kick it, kid!

Kick it!
Kick it!
Kick it, kid!

Kick it!
Kick it!
Kick it, kid!

League Fatigue

Our side is sliding down the league.
So, maestro, meet our meagre need;
Some lullabies by Brahms . . . or Grieg
To lull away our dull fatigue,
Or lieder . . . they would do indeed
To lift our listless league fatigue.

We're suffering from league fatigue
While slipping down the football league,
So, doctor, doctor, dear colleague,
Prescribe some drug which will blitzkrieg
The bug behind this germ intrigue
That's left us all with league fatigue.

League fatigue . . . . league fatigue . . .
That's left us all with league fatigue.

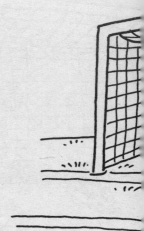

Spectators

They bark instructions, brief and blunt:
'Move!' 'Take him on!' 'Get in front!'
'Left, Kev!' 'Bad luck!' 'Run him, Chaz!'
'Get on!' 'Get your head up, Daz!'
'Get it! Get it! Get it!' 'Shoot!'
'In there, Brian!' 'Use your boot!'
'Wooooooo!' 'Unlucky!' 'Come on, Town!'
'That's a corner!' 'Ref! He's down!'
'On your feet!' 'Don't hang about!'
'Get it out, lads!' 'Get it out!'
'Off side, referee, you berk!'
'Hey there, linesman! Dirty work!'
'Off! Off! Off! Off!' 'Get the ball!'
'Give him some support there, Paul!'
'Yeahhh!' 'Go on!' 'Work 'em well!'
'Free kick!' 'Take it!' 'Give 'em hell!'
'Make some chances!' 'Hey! Off side!'
'Run him, Robbie!' 'Ohhhh, well tried!'
'Good header!' 'In there!' 'Play!'
'Get across him!' 'That's the way!'
'Got it!' 'Squeeze!' 'Now, put it in!'
'Get there, Gary!' 'Gooooooal . . . !'

'We win!'

What Happened to James

Past the goalie James aims
But a tackle lames James.

"Penalty!" exclaims James
But the ref then blames James.

Which is what inflames James,
"That's not fair!" so claims James.

Rage then overcame James
Rudeness soon became names.

Ref decides to tame James
And his red card shames James.

Hunched up sad, that frames James.
"You'll play no more games, James."

A Limerick for the Losing Side

For those who support Man United,
It's easy to get quite excited;
But with lesser teams
It's all hopes and dreams
That, during the season, are blighted.

Jeff the Ref

Old Jeff the ref
Says he's deaf deaf deaf
To the cries cries cries
That arise rise rise
Oh so loud loud loud
From the crowd crowd crowd.

They go, "Foul! Foul! Foul!"
How they howl howl howl
And they growl growl growl
And they scowl scowl scowl
But the nerd nerd nerd
Hasn't heard heard heard
Not a word word word
Not a dickiebird.

'Cos Jeff the ref
Says he's deaf deaf deaf
To the cries cries cries
That arise rise rise
Oh so loud loud loud
From the crowd crowd crowd.

They go boo boo boo
Yes, they do do do
'Cos it's true true true
That a new new new
Referee ree ree
They agree gree gree
Has to be be be
What they need to see.

'Cos Jeff the ref
Says he's deaf deaf deaf
To the cries cries cries
That arise rise rise
Oh so loud loud loud
From the crowd crowd crowd.

Sing along long long
With their song song song
Sing it strong strong strong,
"Ref is wrong wrong wrong!
Chuck him out out out!"
They've no doubt doubt doubt
They all shout shout shout,
"Better off without."

'Cos Jeff the ref
Says he's deaf deaf deaf
To the cries cries cries
That arise rise rise
Oh so loud loud loud
From the crowd crowd crowd.

Slowly Does It

Nice 'n' slowly
Past the goalie . . .

Bowl it, lowly,
Past the goalie . . .
Slip it, slowly,
Past the goalie . . .

Roly-poly
Past the goalie . . .
Oh, so slowlwy
Past the goalie . . .

Partly . . . wholly . . .
Past the goalie . . .
Crawling slowly
Past the goalie . . .

HOLY MOLY!
Can you believe it?
Now their goalie
Can't retrieve it . . .

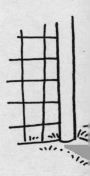

Got the swine!
The ball does fine.
Watch it roll . . .
Over the line . . .

And . . .

Into . . .

The . . .

. . . GOOOOAAAAAALLLLLL!

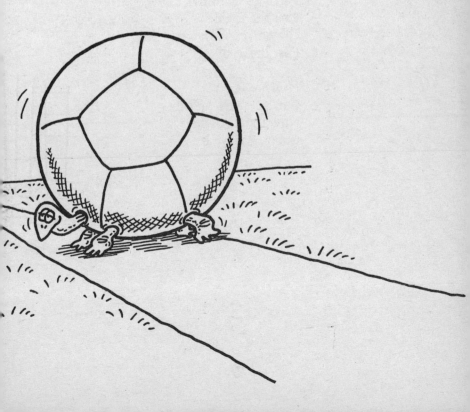

The Substitutes' Bench

The substitutes sit in their kit and their boots
All set to jump up and unzip their track-suits.
They're neutered recruits
Whose sports attributes
Languish, like ungathered fruits.

A Fishy Tale

When the fish found a football, they started a game.
Word spread round the seabed. The fantails all came
Till the carp park was full and they stood shoal-to-shoal,
And it sold out the whole of the Fish Superbowl.
And dogfish on sea horses tried to control
The schools of young hoolie-fish crowding the goal.

When the fish found their football and started that game,
The goldfish were goalies. It's what they became,
Replacing the limpets who'd all limped off lame.
The manatee referee then placed the blame
On the plaice and sent them off. The crowd shouted,
    "Shame!"
And hissed him and called him an unpleasant name.

When the fish found the football which started their game –
The one in the ocean to which fantails came –
Fish packed in like sardines till hardly a sole
Swam in the sea lanes or saw the porthole
Of the trawler that ever-so-silently stole
Up on them all. That's why none could cry, "Goal!"
When the ball hit the net, 'cos the crowd as a whole
Was gutted . . . and served as a fish-supper bowl
In a pub on dry land called The Old Metropole
On the day Town beat City by one splendid goal.

Football Results

The results	1	looks	4
ward	2	reading in	1
's local l	8	edition	2
night are	1	thing	1
ca	0	af	4
d	2	miss. And i	5
had the luck	2	have	1
the pools,	3	son	4
it will be all	2	obvious. "It's a	0
wind . . ." I've of	10	heard them say be	4
about somebody	7	-sent	1
derfully	4	tune	8
win, when every	1	else hasn't	1

(The results one looks forward to reading in one's local late edition tonight are one thing one can ill afford to miss. And if I've had the luck to have won the pools, the reason for it will be all too obvious. "It's an ill wind . . ." I've often heard them say before about somebody's heaven-sent wonderfully fortu-nate win, when everyone else hasn't won.)

OFF!

It's a rough, ill-mannered game
That's played out in this ceaseless drizzle.
Well may you wonder what became
Of sportsmanship, as both sides bristle.

When anger flares up like a flame,
The players' tempers fry and frizzle.
Though calm, the referee's the same.
Provoked, he's prickly as a thistle.

As claim of foul meets counter-claim,
A few fists fly. Some swear-words sizzle.
And if anything'll untame
The man-in-black's composure, this'll.

He knows exactly who's to blame
And he blasts away on his whistle.
"OFF!" That's all he needs to exclaim –
A monosyllabic dismissal.

Saved

The old rogue's dead, but we still rave
About the famous day that Dave
Achieved his most fantastic save . . .

. . . which won the Cup. Wow! Some close shave!
We then gave our Mexican wave
The day Dave made his wondrous save.

So on the slab we laid to pave
The patch of earth above his grave
We paid a mason to engrave:

"Here lies a man whose name was Dave.
Have mercy, Lord, we humbly crave.
He has been known to misbehave.

There's just his body in this grave –
A shell as hollow as a cave.
His soul's been sent for you to save.

And so we pray that you forgave
The sins of this departed knave
Who, just like you, knew how to save."

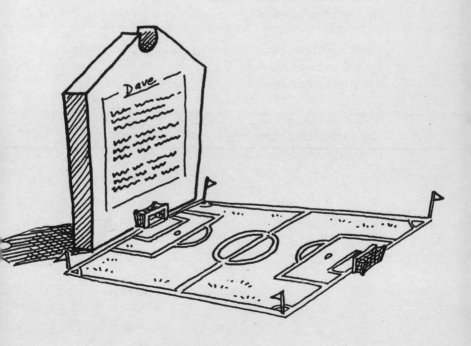

Our Last-Minute Goal

They all thought we wouldn't,
We wouldn't get one,
And said that it couldn't,
It couldn't be done.

The goals we'd put in'd
Be no more than none –
A rumour they shouldn't,
They shouldn't have spun.

'Cos, all of a sudden,
We've suddenly won.
The job is a good'un,
A good'un, my son.

How to Embarrass Teachers

Poems chosen by Paul Cookson

It's time to get even with your teachers!

Ever cringed at something your teacher has said or done?
Then these poems are for you!

Now's the time to find out how a well-placed whoopee
cushion (among other things) can make your teacher
squirm . . .

Biting Mad

I love to make my teacher mad,
I love to make him shout
cos when his tongue gets tangled up
his new false teeth fall out!

Celia Gentles

tHE DOG ATE MY BUSPASS

Poems chosen by
Nick Toczek and Andrew Fusek Peters

A brilliant collection of hilarious poems
featuring some of the world's most incredible
excuses, apologies, tall stories and fibs.
It is essential reading for all children
(and some adults too!).

from The Worst Excuses in the World

by Clare Bevan

I'd only left it for two minutes while I built a scale
model of Buckingham Palace out of cheese triangles,
when a whole herd of angry wildebeest stampeded
through our back garden, battered down the kitchen
door and, before they vanished into the shimmering
sunset, they trampled my book under their mighty,
thundering hoofs, and the dog ate it.

A selected list of titles available from Macmillan Children's Books

The prices shown below are correct at the time of going to press. However, Macmillan Publishers reserves the right to show new retail prices on covers, which may differ from those previously advertised.

The Dog Ate My Bus Pass Nick Toczek and Andrew Fusek Peters	978-0-330-41800-3	£3.99
Can We Have Our Ball Back, Please? Gareth Owen	978-0-330-44048-6	£3.99
How to Embarrass Teachers Paul Cookson	978-0-330-44276-3	£3.99
How to Survive School David Harmer	978-0-330-43951-0	£3.99
The Truth About Teachers Paul Cookson, David Harmer, Brian Moses and Roger Stevens	978-0-330-44723-2	£4.99